Start your own

HOW TO BUY AND SELL MEDICAL SUPPLIES

business

David Powers

Over 116 Million Dollars in Medical Supplies Sold!

Change your life financially with one of the most lucrative small businesses in America! No experience, education or large investment needed!

ISBN 979-8-218-08006-8 (Paperback Edition)
ISBN 979-8-218-08201-7 (E-book Edition)

Printed in the United States of America

First Edition October 2022

www.sellmedsupplies.com

For more information on how you can start your own business buying and selling medical supplies or how you can attend an online live training course with David, please visit

www.sellmedsupplies.com

Contents

About the Author   1

Foreword   3

Preface   5

Introduction   7

Testimonials   9

Questions & Answers   17

Chapter 1:   What You Need to Start Your Business   25

Chapter 2:   Types of Medical (Surgical Supplies)   31

Chapter 3:   Where to Buy Medical Supplies
Avenue One: Medical Facilities
(Hospitals and Surgery Centers)   57

Chapter 4:   Determining the Value
of a Medical Facility's Inventory List   61

Chapter 5:   Where to Buy Medical Supplies
Avenue Two: Medical Auctions   69

Chapter 6:   Types of Auction Endings   73

Chapter 7:   What Not to Buy at Auctions   77

Chapter 8:   Selling Wholesale Versus Retail   79

Chapter 9:   Selling Your Medical Products to   81
              Hospitals and Surgery Centers

Chapter 10:   Selling Your Medical Products to   87
              Other Medical Brokers

Chapter 11:   Developing an Excel Spreadsheet   93
              of Your Inventory

Chapter 12:   Selling Your Medical Products Online   97

Chapter 13:   Pricing Your Medical Products   99

Chapter 14:   Inspecting Your Products Before Selling   103

Chapter 15:   Rotation of Inventory   105

Chapter 16:   Scams to Avoid   107

Chapter 17:   Bookkeeping and Record Keeping   109

Chapter 18:   Accounting Software   113

Online Training   115

Registration   117

Start your own

HOW TO BUY AND
SELL MEDICAL
SUPPLIES

business

About the Author

"I started out my medical career as a sales rep for Arthrex, which is the leading sports medicine company in the world. In 2004, I received the prestigious award of being the top sales rep in the United States out of four hundred and fifty reps.

During this time, I also received two United States patents for medical devices which I, personally, designed and had engineered pertaining to arthroscopic shoulder surgery.

After many years working as a rep, I figured out that I could earn substantially more money by buying and selling surgical supplies for myself instead of making all the money for the company I worked for.

With that being said, I resigned from Arthrex in 2005 to start my own business buying and selling medical supplies. I operated my business very successfully from 2005 until I semi-retired in 2017.

During that time period, I maintained an A+ rating with the Better Business Bureau and sold over $116 million dollars in medical supplies, which averaged out to be $8.9 million dollars in sales per year with an annual *profit* of just over $4 million dollars per year.

I quickly realized how easy this business was to learn and how profitable it truly is. Of course, I made my share of mistakes by buying some of the wrong items or by paying too much for them.

About the Author

However, making mistakes and learning from those mistakes is how a person becomes more knowledgeable and successful.

So, with this guide, I teach you everything you need to do, to know, and, more importantly, I teach you how to avoid the mistakes I made.

I am actually very proud to have written this book, because I know it will help people change their lives financially and, to sum it up in one word, how that makes me feel...*priceless!*"

Wishing everyone success,

David Powers

Foreword

Imagine making more money than you know what to do with while having the freedom to work when you want and take vacations when you want. Owning your own medical sales business gives you that luxury and freedom!

You do _NOT_ need any type of medical experience or college degree.

You do _NOT_ need any special type of license.

You do _NOT_ need any type of knowledge of medical procedures.

You do _NOT_ need a large bankroll to start.

Learn step-by-step from America's foremost expert with 17 years' experience. Follow his methods and you will be successful with financial freedom beyond your belief.

This is the first and *only* guide available in the United States.

In this guide, you will learn:

- How to buy excess medical supplies from hospitals and surgery centers

- How to buy medical supplies from auctions

- How to resell medical supplies to hospitals and surgery centers

- How to resell medical supplies online (eBay and other sites)

- Which medical supplies to buy, not to buy, and so much more

Preface

Although this guidebook contains everything you need to know in order to start your own business buying and selling medical supplies, I have found that some people would like further training. Therefore, I, personally, offer a 6 hour live online training course every other month for a very minimal fee.

At the end of this guidebook, you will find the course registration page. Simply tear it out of this guidebook, complete the information and send the form to the address provided on the page.

Available course dates are listed online on my website at www.sellmedsupplies.com. Registration is also available online.

Thank you,

David Powers

Introduction

I'm sure you have heard at least once in your life that people selling medical supplies earn a ton of money. Well, that is absolutely a true statement. In fact, it is one of the most lucrative small businesses in America.

Let me shed some light on a few things:

People, in general, are nervous to make a change in their lives and this is especially true when it comes to changing jobs or starting their own business. Most (not all) people are paid little money with their current job. Their current job demands a lot of hours and has little vacation time. How and why people are content living their lives like that; I really don't understand.

The amount of money people make selling medical supplies is substantial. You may think buying and selling medical supplies is difficult, but on the contrary, it is extremely easy.

The only reason you feel that way is because you probably don't know much about the medical sales business. Ask anyone who is financially successful, and they will tell you they got that way by taking a chance in life!

Ask yourself these questions:

Do I want to earn more money?

Do I want to work less hours?

Do I want to take more vacations?

Do I want to spend more time with family and friends?

To be blunt, anyone with common sense is going to answer, "Yes," to those questions. The real question should be... how do I obtain all of that? Well, the simple answer is to follow this guide step-by-step as you take advantage of my personal experience and knowledge.

Here is my suggestion for anyone who is hesitant to start their own business: You do *not* need to quit your current job.

What you *can* do is slowly build your medical sales business from your home or office (if you don't want to rent a warehouse) until your income reaches the point that you feel comfortable quitting your current job or you can keep your current job and sell medical supplies as a secondary income.

Testimonials

Prior to writing this book, I offered live in-person and online training courses on how to buy and sell medical supplies. I am proud to say that it was with great success. Here are just a few of the many testimonials I received from my former students.

"I came across David's ad the first part of March and gave him a call about his opportunity. As I am a super skeptical person, I vetted David with no mercy. Not only did he answer all questions to my satisfaction, but he also seemed very genuine, which is very hard to find anywhere!

After doing due diligence on the things we discussed, my wife and I decided that I should invest in the training. Not only was the training exactly like David had stated but, I, actually, sold my first item on the fourth day I was back at home.

I'm a believer in David and the process and I would encourage any person with an entrepreneurial spirit to take advantage of this man's knowledge. Do exactly what he teaches, invest in the inventory you can afford and start making money. Thanks David!"

- Ed Evans

"Unbelievable is the best way to describe what David Powers has done for myself and my family. At first, I was skeptical (as who wouldn't be now a days when you see a business opportunity that seems *too good to be true*).

I decided to take a chance with the training course offered by David Powers, and it turned out to be the best financial decision I ever made in my life.

Only seven months after taking his course, I quit my full-time job as an accountant and now, have my very own successful medical sales company.

Anyone reading this, I will tell you Mr. Powers is the kindest man I know other than my father. This man truly cares about your life and goes out of his way to help. If you want to be financially set, then take this course and thank God you have the pleasure of crossing paths with Mr. Powers."

- Becky Harris

"I can't thank you enough, David, for how you have positively changed my life financially. I lost pretty much everything due to my divorce and was beyond desperate, months behind in my mortgage and other bills.

I borrowed money from my sister to take your course and to buy medical supply inventory.

In two months from the time that I took your course, I paid back my sister, paid all my past mortgage payments and other overdue bills.

Now, in eight months, I have passed, and I have made enough money to buy my own warehouse which is a blessing considering I started off storing the medical supplies in my garage.

I, now, work three days a week and hired my first employee. Words can't describe how much I am in debt to you for you have truly changed my life.

Thank you from the bottom of my heart, David!"

- Dennis Taylor

"When you hear the word, "medical sales," it sounds complicated, but after taking the training course with Mr. Powers, I couldn't believe how easy it is. He is an amazing teacher who really cares about helping you.

In the beginning, I hired Mr. Powers as a consultant after my training course and I would send him money to buy medical supplies for me to sell. Once I received them, I put them for sale on eBay and it was incredible how quickly items sold. I had Mr. Powers buy my medical supplies for the first three months and then felt comfortable buying them myself after understanding what type of items to buy. It's amazing how many medical supplies are out there to buy.

I strongly suggest hiring Mr. Powers as a consultant to help you with your business for the first three months after you take his training course. He definitely knows what he is doing, and he has changed my life forever".

- Amy Miller

"What can I say about the man who changed my life for the better? There are so many scams out there, that it is difficult to find legitimate people who you can trust.

David Powers is certainly a man who you can trust to help you start your business and, if you do what he teaches you, you will build a legitimate medical sales business. David has a good heart and when you talk to him on the phone, you can sense he cares about you as a person and cares about the success of your company. I'm so thankful to have taken his course."

- Steven Thompson

"When I came across the advertisement for starting your own medical sales business, I called to speak with David Powers, who owns the company.

I had a ton of questions and concerns. After our conversation, I felt completely comfortable with him and he had all the answers I needed, so, I signed up for his class.

Of course, I was nervous because I knew nothing about medical products. Then after taking his course, I realized I didn't need to know anything about what the medical products are or what they are used for. All I had to do was take a photo of the product and read the description on the boxes. Then post them on eBay.

Never in a million years, would I have believed it was so easy until I had seen it for myself.

Thank you, David, and my family thanks you."

- Michael Lewis

"About six months ago, I started my own business with the help and knowledge of David Powers. Now, I work full time for myself. I was able to quit my previous job, fully pay my business bills and mortgage, as well as, make a profit in just four months.

I, currently, have my own warehouse and office with the freedom of being my own boss.

David Powers is vastly experienced in the field of medical products, but he is also extremely savvy in running a business.

He has a quality that many teachers do not; *he cares.*

He does not only just want to teach you how to get into this field, but he also wants you to succeed and create your own stable business doing so. His guidance has led me to be in a position of financial freedom I had only dreamed of.

Starting my company has been life changing; a literal dream come true!"

- Adam Woronecki

"In researching, 'Cost Containment, Inc.' and 'David Powers,' on the internet, I found a lot of information about the company and about him.

Everything I found was positive and showed me this company is the *real deal.*

So, I took his course, and it turned out to be the best decision I ever made (second to marrying my wife, of course).

The amount of money I, now, make selling medical supplies is incredible. I never went to college, and I never graduated from high school, but I did get my GED.

Now, I am the proud owner of my own medical sales company and I make more money than I ever dreamed of."

- Carlos Martinez

Questions & Answers

Question:

How many different books are there available to teach people how to start their own business buying and selling medical supplies?

Answer:

There is only *one* and, ironically, you are holding it in your hand at this very moment.

Question:

Why are you teaching people how to buy and sell medical supplies?

Answer:

I have always wanted to change the world but, simply put, changing the world is not an easy task. However, changing the lives of individuals is very possible. Knowing that I have helped people better their lives financially for themselves and for their families will give me satisfaction of knowing I have made a positive difference in this world.

Question:

Do I need a special license to sell medical supplies?

Answer:

No special license is required except for a state sales tax sellers' permit from your state, which is something every business must have. You are only required to pay state sales tax on the medical supplies you sell which are being shipped to an address within your state.

For example: if you live in Florida, you only pay state sellers' tax if you sell an item that is shipped to a Florida address. If you ship to a customer in Texas, any other state or internationally, you do not pay state sales tax.

Question:

What is the difference between medical supplies and surgical supplies?

Answer:

Surgical supplies are medical supplies which are used in surgical procedures on a patient or in the surgical room at the time the patient is having surgery. Selling surgical supplies is where the most money can be made in this field of business. Products like knee braces, wheelchairs, and crutches are *not* considered surgical supplies. Businesses who sell those types of products do not make a substantial income compared to selling surgical supplies. Surgical supplies are what this book will teach you how to locate, buy and sell.

Question:

Do I need medical training or experience in the medical field or a college degree?

Answer:

Absolutely NOT! It is irrelevant what you are currently doing now for work or what you have done in the past for work. This is more of a hands-on type of business whereas you learn as you go and the more medical and surgical products you sell, the more you learn and the easier this business becomes.

Question:

How much money can I expect to make buying and selling medical and surgical supplies?

Answer:

The amount of medical and surgical supplies available nationwide is pretty much endless and you will *never* have a problem finding inventory to buy. Selling is the easy part but knowing how much to pay for the supplies and what supplies to buy or not to buy is where my training comes in to teach you.

I teach you how to research the supplies to determine their value before you purchase. I provide you with my contacts who will buy the surgical supplies from you. I teach you how to sell them online and, most importantly, I teach you how to make huge profits.

So, to answer your question, I can say if you are not making $30,000.00USD to $100,000.00USD per month, then you are being lazy.

Sorry to say it like that, but I speak the truth to shame the devil. Yes, it seems like a crazy amount of money, but in this type of business, it is not difficult to obtain.

Question:

How and where do I locate medical and surgical supplies to buy?

Answer:

The amount of medical supplies available nationwide is endless. I teach you how to contact hospitals and surgery centers to buy their excess inventory. I teach you who to contact at those facilities, what to say, and how to make offers.

There are also *numerous* medical auctions nationwide every month. I teach you what to buy, what not to buy, and how much to pay for it. I also teach you how to research what those products sell for; which helps you to determine how much to pay for them.

Question:

Can I lose money in this business?

Answer:

Believe it or not, the answer is, "No."

"*If,*" and only if, you do what I train you to do in this guidebook. When I teach you how to research the prices in which products sell for, you obviously buy the products for much less. Therefore, "No. You can't lose your money."

Now, on the other hand, (and to play Devil's advocate), if you buy something without doing the proper research and if you buy items which I advised you not to buy, well, then yes, you can lose money.

The purpose of this guidebook is so you don't make those blatant type of mistakes. So, just follow my guidance and *don't* try to reinvent the wheel.

It's just that simple!

Question:

How much money do I need to start this business?

Answer:

You can pretty much start with any amount and grow your inventory by flipping the products. For example, let's say you have $2,000.00USD to start buying inventory. When you buy products at the right price (which is what this guide teaches you), you can turn that $2,000.00USD into $4,000.00USD then into $15,000.00USD or even more depending on what supplies you buy.

You then reinvest that amount into buying more inventory, aka *supplies*, and pretty soon, you have a large bankroll to buy larger quantities of supplies. The higher bankroll you have, the more buying power you have in order to obtain more inventory for less money dollar for dollar or better known as "*more bang for your buck*." Obviously, the more money you initially have to purchase inventory, the more money you can make and see larger profits from faster. The key is to reinvest your profit into buying more inventory.

Question:
Do I need an office or warehouse?

Answer:
Initially, you will not need one as long as you have a spare room in your home or can use your garage or basement.

First, let's build your inventory and your income. Then after that, you can look into securing an office or warehouse. In the beginning, why spend more money than you need to? That is unless, of course, you simply prefer to have an office or warehouse.

This type of business is not like a storefront. Customers will *not* be going to your house or to your office or warehouse to purchase medical supplies from your business. You will be selling your supplies online and/or directly back into other hospitals and/or surgery centers nationwide and internationally, as well as, to other medical brokers.

Question:
Where do I sell the medical and surgical supplies I purchase?

Answer:
You will be selling them online and/or back into hospitals, surgery centers, as well as, to other medical brokers.

However, if you prefer to only sell the medical products online, that is perfectly fine, too. This guidebook teaches you all aspects and if you chose to sell some products to hospitals and surgery centers, I teach you who to contact at those facilities, how to bill them, how to generate a proper list of products to sell, what type of products they will buy, and so on.

Question:

Do you offer any additional type of training besides what is inside this guidebook?

Answer:

Yes. If you visit my website at www.sellmedsupplies.com or look towards the end of this guidebook, there are instructions on how to register for a one day (6 hour) live online training course. You can also find the registration form towards the end of this guidebook. Simply complete the information, tear it out of this book and return it to the address provided on the registration form. I offer one (6 hour) online live training course per month for a very minimal fee.

1

What You Need
to Start Your Business

Number *1*:

First and foremost, you need to determine how you want to structure your business.

This will be in the form of either a DBA (Doing Business As), which is also referred to as a Sole Proprietorship, Corporation (C-Corp or S-Corp), or a Limited Liability Corporation (LLC).

Let's break each one down to better understand. My advice is to speak to your accountant or tax professional to choose which business structure best fits your needs.

DBA/Sole Proprietorship:

If you choose to go it alone, without incorporating or otherwise establishing a business entity, you are then considered a sole proprietor. This is the easiest form of business to start because you don't need to draft a partnership agreement or register to incorporate.

It is also the least expensive, as a DBA has a minimal application fee. This can be done online, or you can go to your local courthouse and ask for the department for filing a DBA. Normally, it is the Clerk of Courts department.

Even though a DBA/Sole Proprietorship is the easiest type of business to form and the least expensive, it also leaves you more exposed to liability. Meaning, if your business goes into debt or out of business, you can still be held personally liable for debt incurred and/or taxes owed.

You can take out product insurance or take out other forms of insurance to protect yourself, but it may not completely protect you. This is why most people choose to form some type of corporation.

Corporation (C-Corp or S-Corp):

A corporation is a legal entity unto itself. In a corporation, you may have less liability exposure than as a sole proprietor. It is also a legally formed business entity with laws, rules, and guidelines you must follow.

The process of incorporating is done in accordance with your state's laws. I suggest you have an attorney assist you in the process as he/she will have knowledge of state requirements for forming a corporation.

You will also be required to pay a fee to the state for incorporating and must file corporate certificates annually. For a fee, your attorney can handle that aspect for you.

The most significant advantage of incorporating is that it allows your business and personal responsibilities to be handled separately. Therefore, you reduced your personal liability tremendously. You can also leave a corporation without having to dissolve the business, since you and your corporation are

26

separate entities.

Once you incorporate, you pay yourself a salary or a disbursement from the corporation. You also pay corporate taxes as well as your own personal income taxes based on how much salary you pay yourself. Unlike a sole proprietorship, whose profits land on top of his/her taxable income, a corporation pays a separate tax.

In forming a corporation, you will need to choose between an "S-Corp" or a "C-Corp." I suggest speaking with your attorney and or accountant to best determine which of the two best fits your business model and personal needs.

Most small business owners elect to form an "S-Corp," which is known as a "Small Business Corporation". By definition, it is a company that cannot have more than 100 shareholders, which you would definitely fall into that category as a medical sales broker.

An "S-Corp" still provides personal liability protection. However, the profits from the "S-Corp" are not federally taxed but are passed through your personal income and taxed accordingly.

Limited Liability Company (LLC):

A Limited Liability Company, also known as an LLC, is a hybrid type of business structure where the owners of the LLC are called "members," and a business entity with all the protection of a corporation plus the ability to pass through any business profits and losses to your personal income tax return.

Business owners looking for the liability protection that a corporation can provide when starting a business, without the double taxation, should consider forming an LLC. LLC members can be an individual business owner, several partners, or other businesses.

Number 2:

Obtain your Business EIN number
(also known as an Employer Identification Number).

Even if you don't plan on having employees, you are still required to have an EIN number for your business. You can obtain your EIN number online or you can have your attorney obtain it for you.

Number 3:

Open a business checking account.

In order to open a business checking account, you will need to have your EIN number. Every bank will ask you for your EIN number when opening a business checking account.

Number 4:

You will need a reliable computer, preferably a desktop.

Number 5:

Establish an eBay account if you don't already have one.

If you plan to sell medical supplies online, you will need to link your bank account to your eBay account so that you can receive payments from eBay for the supplies you sell.

In the past, eBay customers (buyers) would pay through PayPal, but eBay now has what is called, "eBay Managed

Payments," and what that means is that eBay directly deposits all payments into your bank account instead of into PayPal.

_N_umber _6_:

You will need the following miscellaneous supplies: Digital camera, blank 3" x 5" index cards, black sharpies, and scotch tape.

Note: You may or may not choose to rent an office or warehouse. That is totally your choice. Initially, you really don't need one as long as you have a room in your home to put up some shelves which can be purchased from Home Depot or Lowes, or you may use your basement or garage. As you grow your inventory, then you may consider securing an office/warehouse.

Furthermore, I have had many people ask me if they should design a website. Again, this is something you may consider down the road, but it is not necessary being that you will be selling supplies online, such as, on eBay or directly to hospitals, surgery centers or other medical brokers.

*N*umber 7:

Register as a user with www.terapeak.com.

This is only needed if you are planning to sell medical products online with eBay or Dotmed. This Terapeak site is a research platform linked to eBay.

What it allows you to do is search back twelve months of eBay sales to find out if a specific product has ever sold on eBay. If it has sold, it will show you how many products sold over

twelve months along with how much each product sold for and how much the seller charged for shipping. This will show you how much you can receive for the medical item.

Terapeak is not just used for researching medical supplies. It can be used to research any type of product such as home goods, sporting goods, vehicles, outdoor equipment, and any other type of product. The Terapeak website is vital to selling medical items on eBay.

2

Types of Medical
(Surgical) Supplies

The term, "Medical Supplies," is very broad and ranges greatly in resale value. The medical supplies with the highest value are surgical products.

What are surgical products? They are defined as products used in the operating room to facilitate the surgical procedure on a patient. For example: A patient is having a surgical procedure to repair his or her rotator cuff or maybe he or she needs a vascular stent put in due to heart problems. Both of those are called "implants." Of course, the surgeon has to use some sort of instrument to put the implant into the patient, which are called, "Surgical Instruments."

Now, I am sure you have heard of people selling medical supplies, such as, wheelchairs, walkers, crutches, braces, and so on. Yes, they are classified as medical products, but they are low value items and *not* items used in surgical procedures.

Those type of products you can, of course, sell; but don't expect to make a huge profit doing so. I, myself, don't waste my time selling low value items and I suggest you don't either.

Surgical supplies can be classified into three categories which I will, now, break down for you to better understand.

*C*ategory *1*:

Implants and/or Disposables

These are a one-time use product in surgery. For example, a screw and a plate to fix a broken bone or a stent for heart surgery.

There are thousands of examples, but the main point is that it is a *"sterile"* product that can be used one time in surgery and then the medical facility would have to buy another one to replace it for the next time that product is needed for surgery.

These types of products are also referred to as *"consumables."* If you would like to see an example online, type the words, "Ethicon HAR36," into a Google search. You will then find pictures of this product online. Notice that the product is contained inside a package or a box. Reason being this product has been packaged and sterilized by the manufacturer which is ready to be used in surgery as long as the expiration date has not passed. If the expiration date has passed, then no medical facility in the United States can legally use that product in surgery.

However, this now expired product still has value and can be used legally in foreign countries. Actually, there is a *huge* market for international buyers who actively seek expired products because it saves their hospitals money, and they will actually re-sterilize the product prior to using in surgery.

Here are some other product codes to type into a Google search to get a better understanding of implants and/or disposables. Again, also known as *consumables*.

Manufacturer	Product Code	Product Name
Arthrex	AR-7200	Fiberwire
Arthrex	AR-13990N	Scorpion Needle
Arthrex	AR-1920SF	Corkscrew Anchor
Covidien	LF4418	Ligasure
Covidien	176643	Endo Shears
Covidien	111987	Stapler
Ethicon	GST60B	Vascular Staple Reload
Ethicon	HAR36	Shears
Ethicon	B12LT	Trocar
Bard	0010303	Hernia Mesh
Zimmer	00-1118-140-01	Bone Cement
Maquet	095307	Vascular Graft

There are hundreds of manufacturers and hundreds of thousands of products on the market, so, above, are just a few examples.

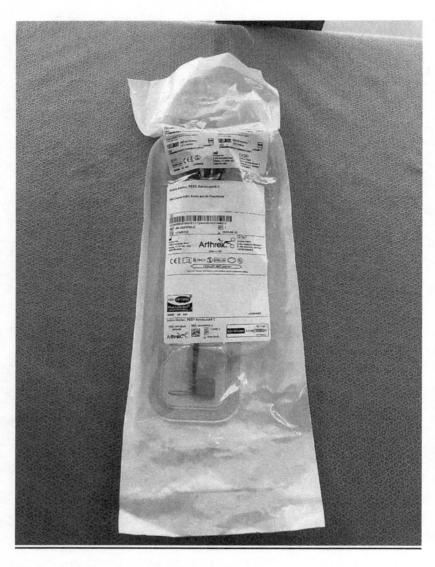

Category 1: Implants and Disposables

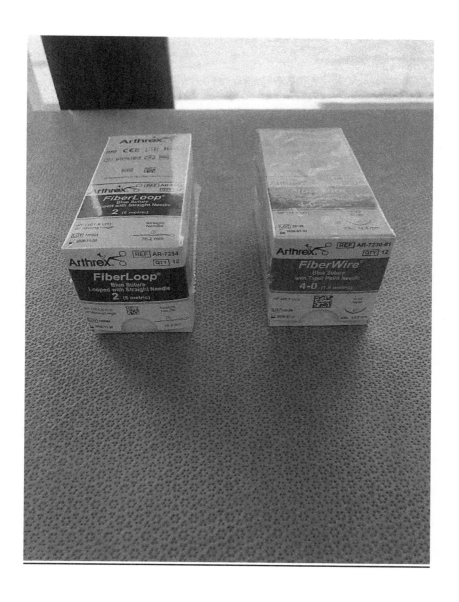

Category 1: Implants and Disposables

Category 1: Implants and Disposables

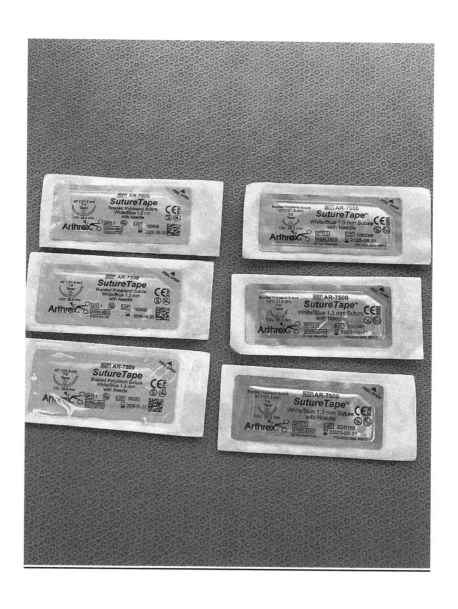

Category 1: Implants and Disposables

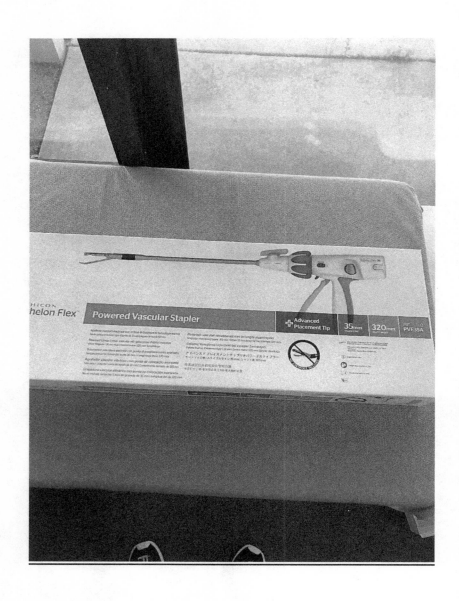

Category 1: Implants and Disposables

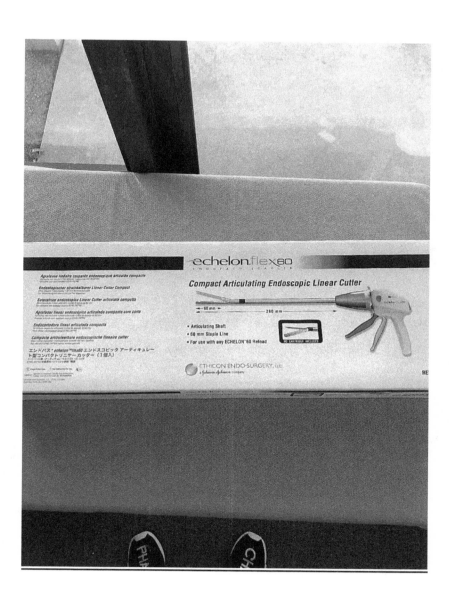

Category 1: Implants and Disposables

*C*ategory *2*:

Instruments

Instruments are the actual tools a surgeon uses to perform the surgery. Just like a mechanic has tools to fix your car or a plumber has tools to fix your plumbing, a surgeon has tools to fix your body.

The only real difference is that the hospital will pay $500.0USD for a screwdriver and you can buy the same looking screwdriver at Home Depot for $10.00USD. Now, do you see why this business is so lucrative.

Instruments are *not* a one-time use product and, almost always, they are made of titanium or stainless steel. After the surgeon uses the instruments in surgery, those instruments are sent down to central processing to be cleaned and re-sterilized for the next surgery.

There are hundreds of thousands of different types of surgical instruments being that every type of surgical procedure uses different types of instruments. Not to sound redundant, but a car mechanic has hundreds of instruments and tools, whereas, using different tools based on what he needs to fix on a vehicle.

For a visual example, type into a Google search the words, "Arthrex AR-13990," which you will then see an instrument called a, "Scorpion Suture Passer." This is an example of a surgical instrument.

Here are some other product codes to type into a Google search to get a better understanding of what surgical instruments look like.

Manufacturer	Product Code	Product Name
Arthrex	AR-12000	Biter
Arthrex	AR-13255	Suture Cutter
Arthrex	AR-1486	Screwdriver
Karl Storz	27175A	Alligator Grasper
Stryker	6710-210-020	Bipolar Forcep
Synthes	323.36	Drill Guide
Synthes	391.98	Plate Cutter
Codman	36-2018	Needle Holder
Aesculap	FB836R	Rib Spreader
Aesculap	BT552R	Abdominal Retractor

There are hundreds of manufacturers and hundreds of thousands of products on the market, so above, are just a few examples.

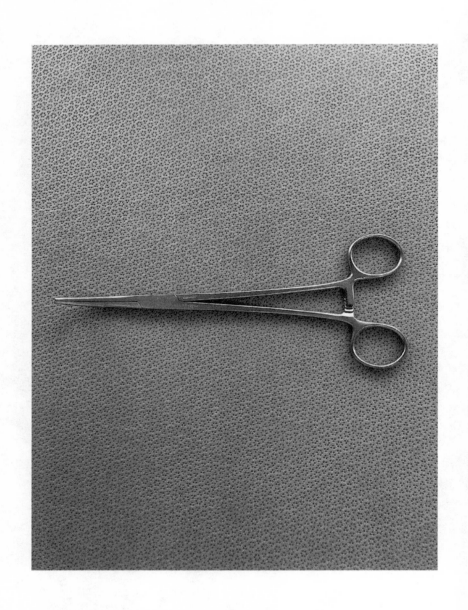

Category 2: Instruments

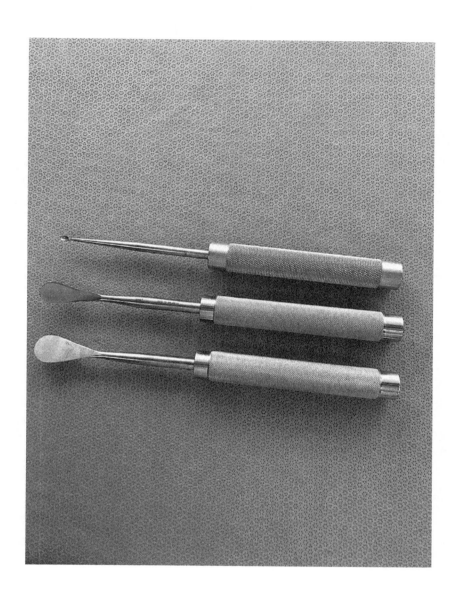

Category 2: Instruments

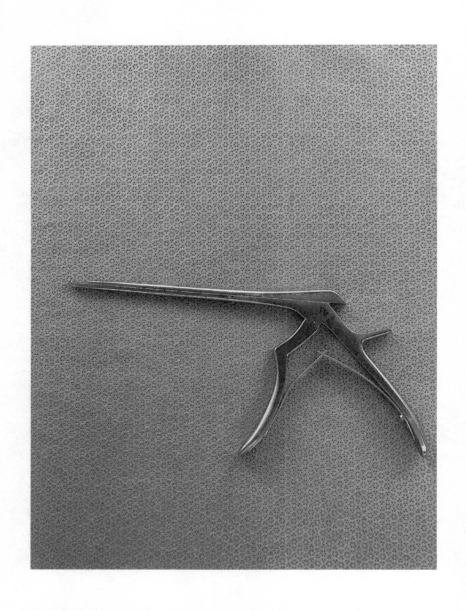

Category 2: Instruments

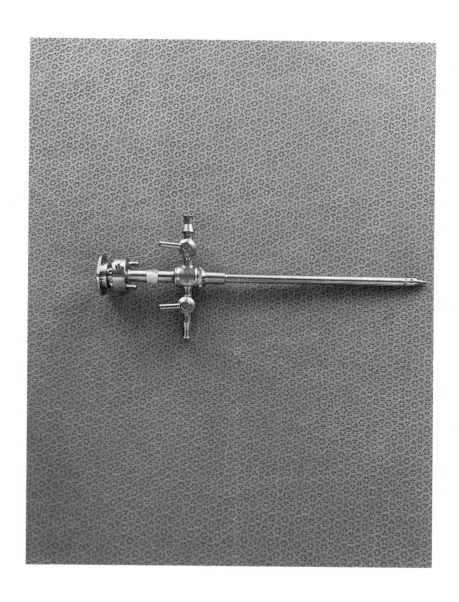

Category 2: Instruments

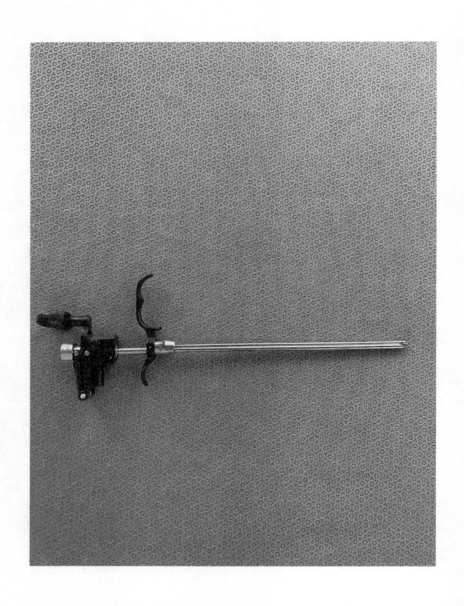

Category 2: Instruments

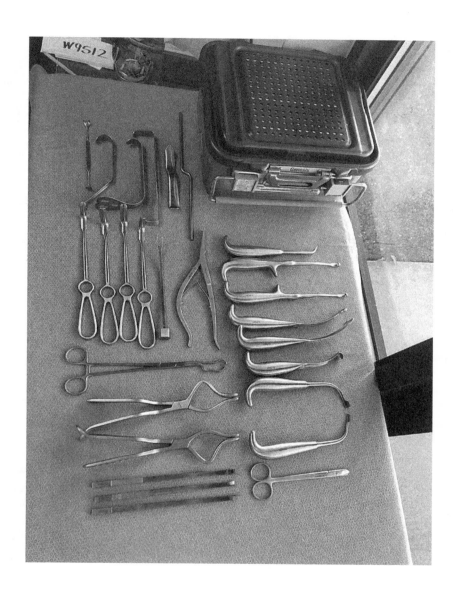

Category 2: Instruments

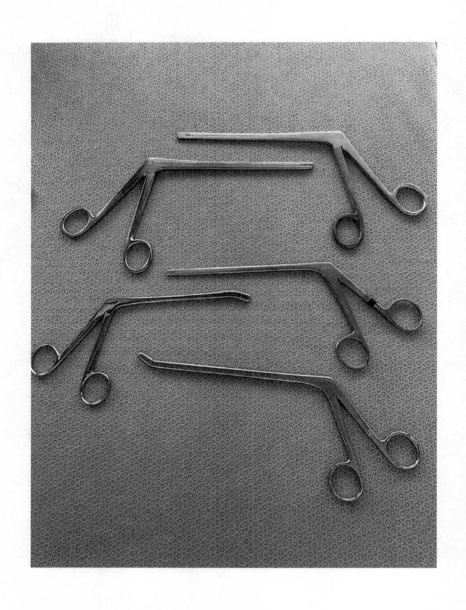

Category 2: Instruments

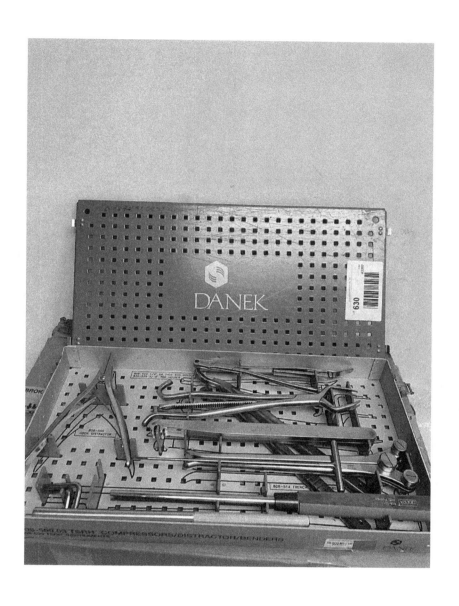

Category 2: Instruments

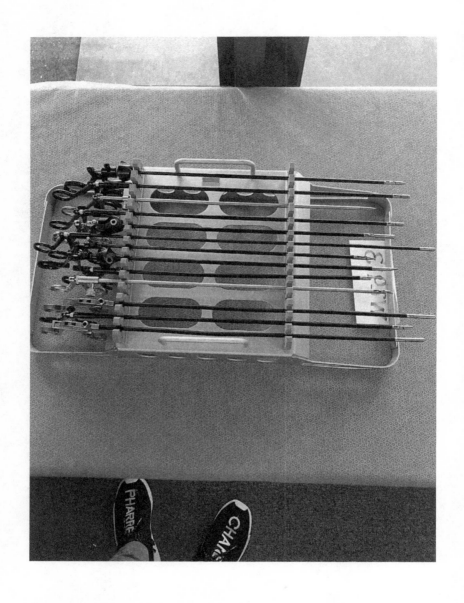

Category 2: Instruments

*C*ategory *3.*

Equipment

This is a very large and broad field. It can range from Operating Room Tables to MRI Machines to Cat Scans to just about anything that, again, pertains to the operating room.

Now, you may think that a Cat Scan, MRI Machine, or an Ultrasound Machine are not used in surgery; and you would be correct.

However, they are equipment that the surgeon will request the patient to be examined with and, therefore, are considered equipment used by or ordered to be used by a surgeon.

Example: a patient is complaining of severe shoulder pain. The surgeon would then, most likely, request for the patient to have an MRI Scan of his or her shoulder to determine if, maybe, there is a rotator cuff tear, labral tear, or some kind of impingement that would then require a surgical procedure to repair.

In the actual operating room, equipment would be considered items such as an Anesthesia Machine, Cameras, Scopes, Operating Room Table, Patient Positioners, Power Tools, and numerous other items.

Here are some other product codes to type into google to get a better understanding of what surgical equipment looks like.

Manufacturer	Product Code	Product Name
Arthrex	AR-1600M	Shoulder Positioner
Arthrex	AR-6529S	Hip Distraction System
Karl Storz	7219BA	Rigid Scope
Karl Storz	11278AU1	Flexible Scope
Olympus	CLV-S40	Light Source
Olympus	OTV-S7	Camera System Console
Olympus	CH-S190-XZ-E	Camera Head
Datex Ohmeda	Aespire 7100	Anesthesia Machine

There are hundreds of manufacturers and hundreds of thousands of products on the market, so above, are just a few examples.

Category 3: Equipment

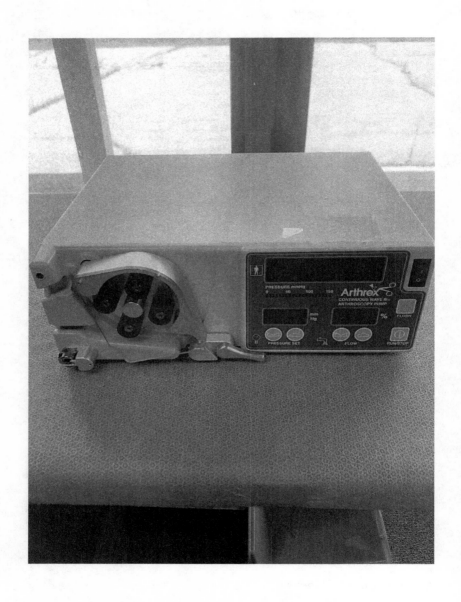

Category 3: Equipment

Category 3: Equipment

Now, that you have a better understanding of the three categories of surgical supplies, I would say the best two to concentrate on buying and selling are the "Instruments," and the "Implants/Disposables."

Reason being that they are the easiest to find and with the highest profit margin. As I also mentioned previously in the guide, the majority of equipment needs a power source to turn on and run.

Therefore, you run the risk of buying it and it doesn't work, which would result in either losing money or having to repair it. That would cut drastically into your profit margin.

3

Where to Buy Medical Supplies

Avenue One:
Medical Facilities
(Hospitals and Surgery Centers)

There are two different avenues to locate and purchase medical supplies. With the amount of excess medical supplies throughout the United States, finding supplies is never a problem.

What initially determines where you buy your supplies will depend on the amount of money you have available to spend on purchasing inventory.

If your current bankroll to purchase inventory is less than $25,000.00USD, then I suggest you, initially, start out buying medical products from medical auctions. Reason being auctions don't require you to buy a specific amount of items. In fact, you can buy only one item if you want.

Of course, you can also buy as many items as you like, which will come down to how much money you have available to spend and how many items you are the highest bidder on. (Remember, you must be the highest bidder to win the item(s) at a medical auction or any auction, so to speak.

If your current bankroll is over $25,000.00USD, (and I would like to say, "closer to $50,000.00USD,"), you can, then, contact hospitals and surgery centers to buy their unwanted or excess supplies.

Why do you need a higher bankroll to do this? Well, it's because most medical facilities have huge amounts of supplies that they want to get rid of, which, of course, requires you to have a higher bankroll (initial investment) to purchase.

Don't worry if your initial bankroll to purchase inventory is minimal. Everyone has to start somewhere.

Simply put, you can start out buying a few items at medical auctions. Then, sell those items for a good profit. Re-invest that money into buying more items at medical auctions until you have built a large enough bankroll to contact medical facilities to buy their large supplies in bulk.

*A*venue *1*:

There are over 14,000 hospitals and surgery centers throughout the United States. On a regular basis, they all have supplies they need to get rid of.

This could be due to the products being expired, having short expiration dates, or the hospital switched over to another manufacturer. Regardless as to their reason, it is an opportunity for you to buy them.

The main person to contact at a hospital or surgery center is the "Materials Manager," and the second person to contact is the "Purchasing Agent."

Depending on the medical facility, one of those two contacts will be in charge of buying medical products for their facility.

The first step is to call the medical facility, whereas most times than not, the main facility operator will answer and ask to whom you would like to speak to.

At that point, you would ask to be transferred to the "Materials Manager." Once that person answers the phone, below, I have laid out a short *to the point* introduction after you two have exchanged the typical, "Hello, how are you?" greetings.

"My name is *(your name)* and my company is *(name of your company)*. The purpose of my call is to inquire as to if you currently have any excess surgical supplies not being used by your facility. My company specializes in helping medical facilities sell their unwanted medical supplies to help them recoup some of the money they initially paid for them. All I would need from you is an inventory list of the products you would like to sell and, from there, I can get you a quote to purchase within a few days."

If the "Materials Manager" or "Purchasing Agent" agrees to provide a list of inventory, be sure to give your email and have that person read it back to you.

I would also suggest exchanging names and to verify the spelling, and same goes for the direct phone number. This is to avoid any mistakes which, in turn, could result in you losing the deal.

Always cross your T's and dot your I's.

To locate and contact hospitals and surgery centers, you can simply Google search the ones in your city. However, don't just limit yourself to contacting the ones in your city or state. You can buy supplies from hospitals and surgery centers anywhere in the United States. If you only concentrate on facilities in your area, you are greatly reducing your ability to find a large lucrative deal, which could be on the other side of the country.

I, initially, started my medical sales company in New York back in 2005 and the majority of my large deals came from medical facilities in California, Texas, and Florida. I would either fly there to, then, rent a large U-Haul truck and, personally, drive the supplies back to New York or I would hire a shipping company to do it for me. I would suggest contacting a mailing list company such as FirstMark, Inc (PH: 800-729-2600) and buy a mailing list from them for all hospitals and surgery centers in the United States. The list will cost a couple thousand dollars, but it will be well worth it.

When contacting FirstMark, you will ask for a complete list of hospitals and surgery centers in the United States broken down by state. You will also want to request the list containing phone numbers and addresses.

Do *not* pay an additional cost for "Contact Names" at the hospitals and surgery centers. Reason being people change jobs or departments on a regular basis.

Therefore, the contact names will not be accurate, and you would not look professional asking for the wrong person when you call. Instead, when you call the medical facility, you will simply ask to speak to the "Materials Manager" or ask to speak to the "Purchasing Agent" if the medical facility, for some reason, does not have a dedicated Materials Manager.

4

Determining the Value of a Medical Facility's Inventory List

Once you receive the "List of Inventory" that the medical facility wants to sell, the next step is to determine the value. This is called the "Market Value" and it is the price you are able to resell each item for on the secondary market.

When medical facilities buy directly from the manufacturer, it is called, "Direct Purchasing." When medical facilities buy medical supplies from brokers, such as yourself, it is called the "Secondary Market."

To determine the market value of the list of items that the medical facility is selling, you can do this in a combination of ways.

First, you can refer to your competitor's websites to see the prices in which they sell the same products. Below are the top medical brokers *(your competitors)* in the country:

Medical Broker	Website
Ringle Medical Supply	ringlemedicalsupply.com

Palm Harbor Medical	palmharbormedical.com
West Coast Medical Supplies	westcmr.com
MTM Medical	mtmmedical.net
Surgical Product Solutions	shopsps.com
eSutures	esutures.com
SH Medical	shmedical.com
Medical Materials	medicalmaterials.com

Second, you can refer to eBay in order to see if anyone is currently selling the same product.

Third, you can refer to the website, www.medwow.com, and within the site, you can click on "Market Value Calculator." This will allow you to search the products by category, device, manufacturer, and model.

Fourth, you can Google search the product to see who is selling it and for what price.

Once you have located pricing for all or most of the items on the Inventory list sent to you by the medical facility, you can, then, add up the total amount in which you can sell the products for on the secondary market.

The following three Excel spreadsheets are examples of a list of supplies a hospital sends you, which they would like you to make an offer to purchase. Sometimes, when you receive lists from hospitals or surgery centers, they will contain the prices they paid for each item and, sometimes, they will not include those prices.

Either way, it doesn't matter, being what a hospital or surgery center paid for their inventory is irrelevant. What you only care about is how much you can sell each item for. With that being said, here is a description of the following three Excel spreadsheets:

1) Excel spreadsheet #1 containing a list of supplies a hospital or surgery center wants to sell to you.

2) Excel spreadsheet #2 showing those products and, after doing research, you filled in the prices that you know you can receive for each product on the secondary market.

3) Excel spreadsheet #3 showing those products and after doing research, you filled in the prices that you know you can receive for each product on the secondary market. However, notice that on this spreadsheet, you were not able to find pricing for some of the products.

Note: It is perfectly okay if you are not able to find your selling price for each product. What you do then, is make an offer to purchase the entire list *only* basing your offer on the products you were able to determine your selling prices. Products that you couldn't find pricing for, you simply consider it a *zero-dollar* value.

Keep in mind that when you make your offer to the hospital or surgery center, you are making a bulk price offer for the *entire* list. You do *not* send them an individual price offer for each item. This is called making a *"Bulk Purchase."*

Below is the list of products a hospital may have sent you to make an offer to purchase.

Excel Spreadsheet #1:

MANUFACTURER	PRODUCT CODE	QUANTITY (UNITS)
Arthrex	AR-13995N	2
Arthrex	AAR-1934BF	4
Arthrex	AR-1662BC	3
Arthrex	AR-8979DS	1
Ethicon	PPH03	4
Ethicon	CHD33A	7
Ethicon	ECS33A	6
Ethicon	EC45A	8
Ethicon	PCEE60A	1
Ethicon	CDH23P	4
Covidien	HEM3335	2
Covidien	EEA28	2
Covidien	EGIAUSTND	5
Covidien	173052	1
Covidien	20242	2
Covidien	ABSTACK30	6
Covidien	92001	3
Covidien	EGIAUXL	8

Below is the same list which, after doing your research, you have determined what price you can sell each product for.

Excel Spreadsheet #2:

MANUFACTURER	PRODUCT CODE	QUANTITY (UNITS)	YOUR SELLING UNIT PRICE EACH	TOTAL PRICE
Arthrex	AR-13995N	2	$140.00	$280.00
Arthrex	AAR-1934BF	4	$200.00	$800.00
Arthrex	AR-1662BC	3	$208.00	$624.00
Arthrex	AR-8979DS	1	$375.00	$375.00
Ethicon	PPH03	4	$380.00	$1,520.00
Ethicon	CHD33A	7	$190.00	$1,330.00
Ethicon	ECS33A	6	$200.00	$1,200.00
Ethicon	EC45A	8	$345.00	$2,760.00
Ethicon	PCEE60A	1	$350.00	$350.00
Ethicon	CDH23P	4	$290.00	$1,160.00
Covidien	HEM3335	2	$350.00	$700.00
Covidien	EEA28	2	$175.00	$350.00
Covidien	EGIAUSTND	5	$300.00	$1,500.00
Covidien	173052	1	$200.00	$200.00
Covidien	20242	2	$70.00	$140.00
Covidien	ABSTACK30	6	$400.00	$2,400.00
Covidien	92001	3	$100.00	$300.00
Covidien	EGIAUXL	8	$300.00	$2,400.00
				$18,389.00

As you look at the above spreadsheet you will see the total value of the list is $18,389.00USD, which is the amount you are able to sell the products for.

Based on that amount, I would suggest offering the hospital 20% of that price which is $3,677.00USD (forget the loose change).

Hopefully, the hospital accepts your offer. The reason for only offering 20% of the list value is two-fold.

First, you are hoping the hospital accepts your offer, whereas you then make a very large return on your investment.

Second, if the hospital turns down your offer, you can then start negotiating by offering the hospital more money. It is best to start low and hope for the best. Starting out low gives you room to move up *(negotiate)*. Raising your offer 10% each time is a good formula.

Below is the exact same spreadsheet but *notice* that you couldn't find pricing for five of the products. This is perfectly okay and normal. You won't always be able to find pricing on every item all the time.

On this list, you determine your resale value to be $12,949.00USD, which you would then offer the hospital 20% for a total offer of $ 2,848.00USD.

Again, you are making an offer on the entire list which is called a *"bulk offer."* You do *not* need to mention to the hospital that you cannot find resale value on some of the items. The hospital only cares about how much money you are offering.

Now, in regard to the five line items and products which you could not initially find prices for on the secondary market. In time, you will either find the pricing on a competitor's website or when you start contacting hospitals or surgery centers, one of them will be using those products and then they will tell you what they normally pay for those items from the manufacturer. Which you would then offer those products to the medical facility at a discount.

Keep in mind, you received those products in the *"bulk offer,"* whereas, you didn't place any value on them so that means you receive 100% profit on those items.

Excel Spreadsheet #3:

MANUFACTURER	PRODUCT CODE	QUANTITY (UNITS)	YOUR SELLING UNIT PRICE EACH	TOTAL PRICE
Arthrex	AR-13995N	2	$140.00	$280.00
Arthrex	AAR-1934BF	4	$200.00	$800.00
Arthrex	AR-1662BC	3	$208.00	$624.00
Arthrex	AR-8979DS	1	$375.00	$375.00
Ethicon	PPH03	4	$380.00	$1,520.00
Ethicon	CHD33A	7	$190.00	$1,330.00
Ethicon	ECS33A	6	$200.00	$1,200.00
Ethicon	EC45A	8	$345.00	$2,760.00
Ethicon	PCEE60A	1	$350.00	$350.00
Ethicon	CDH23P	4	$290.00	$1,160.00
Covidien	HEM3335	2	$350.00	$700.00
Covidien	EEA28	2	$175.00	$350.00
Covidien	EGIAUSTND	5	$300.00	$1,500.00
Covidien	173052	1	?	$0.00
Covidien	20242	2	?	$0.00
Covidien	ABSTACK30	6	?	$0.00
Covidien	92001	3	?	$0.00
Covidien	EGIAUXL	8	?	$0.00
				$12,949.00

5

Where to Buy Medical Supplies

Avenue Two:
Medical Auctions

_A_venue _2_:

Medical auctions are the fastest and easiest way for you to buy excess medical products. Every single month out of the year, there are medical auctions throughout the United States. In fact, there are anywhere between 8-20 medical auctions per month.

Most auctions you must register for in order to bid on items for sale. This is normal and, more often than not, it is a requirement.

Some auctions will require a minimal deposit via your credit card. If you end up winning some of the items you bid on, the deposit will be applied to your purchase. If you spend less that your deposit, then the balance will be refunded back to your credit card. If you spend more than your initial deposit, then you will have to pay the balance before you are given authorization to pick up the medical supplies you purchased.

When it comes to picking up your items, you have the option of picking up the items in person or hiring a packing or shipping company to do it for you.

Most auctions companies provide a list of packing or shipping companies in their area for you to call. If you don't see a list of companies, then call the auction company, as they will be very helpful to provide that information.

I have found that most of the auctions are in larger cities and, more times than not, I simply call the "UPS Store." Most UPS Stores will go to the auction site to pick up your items, pack them, and ship to you. Be sure you Google search the "UPS Stores" in the area of the auction location; *not* a "UPS Hub." The hubs are not a "Pack-N-Ship" service.

If you take the route of having a company pick up your supplies, you will need to fax or email over to them a paid in full receipt from the auction company and a pickup authorization form.

This form is generally downloadable from the auction, or you can call the auction company to have them email you a copy. The reason why auction companies require a pickup authorization form is so that nobody can take your items without your permission. Basically, it is to protect you and your investment.

When the auction has ended, the auction company will send you an invoice for the items you won. Be sure to look it over carefully. You want to make sure that the invoice has all of the "Lot Numbers" of the items that you won and, at the same time, you want to make sure that the auction company did not accidentally put an item (also known as a lot number) on your invoice that you did not win. If you find any mistakes, simply call the auction company to rectify the problem.

Anytime you buy items from an auction, you will want to read the terms and conditions set forth by the auction. This will clearly lay out things such as location of the auction, start date, and end date of the auction, inspection date, (if you would like to, personally, go look at the items before you start bidding), removal dates, and buyers' premium.

It is important to always know what buyers' premium percentage the auction company is charging you and other buyers.

For example: The auction company specifies a 10% buyers' premium. That means once the auction is over, they will add up how much you spent and then the auction company will tack on an additional 10% to your bill.

So, let's say you spent $5,000.00USD at the auction. Your actual bill will be $5,000.00USD plus $500.00USD (10% buyers' premium) for a total bill of $5,500.00USD.

Auction companies may or may not charge state taxes in addition to the buyers' premium. This is something you will need to determine by reading the terms and conditions posted by each auction.

6

Types of Auction Endings

There are only three ways an auction will end.

The first two ways are applicable if the auction is an online auction. Almost all auctions have a terms and conditions page for bidders to review. There, you will find two ways the auction will end, which will either be a "hard" close or a "soft" close.

A "hard" close means when the auction timer runs down to zero, the auction for that lot item has ended with the highest bidder winning the item.

A "soft" close means that once the auction timer for that specific lot item goes below two minutes, if anyone bids, it will extend the auction time on that specific lot number or item, usually by one to three minutes. This is a way for auctions to get more bids on the item, being that some people wait until the last few seconds to bid on the item.

At times, it can be frustrating being you are about to win the item because you are the highest bidder and, just a few seconds before the bid times runs out, another buyer will place a bid; then extending the auction time for that lot number an additional one to three minutes.

This can go on for minutes, or even hours, if the bidding keeps going on. Example: you are the highest bidder. The time runs down to, let's say, ten seconds and then another person places a bid on the item.

Now, instead of there being a few seconds left to the auction time ending for that lot number, the time is now extended to three minutes.

Now, let's say you still want the item and you wait until the time runs down to thirty seconds before you place your next bid on the item. The time will, again, add three minutes to the auction time of that specific lot number.

Again, that can be frustrating, but, in the end, if you win the item and you make a good profit, then that's what matters most:

Making money!

Below, are the main auction companies who hold medical auctions on a regular basis. Most of them hold auctions monthly. However, if you check the internet on a regular basis, you will find other medical auctions that pop up here and there from other less known auction companies.

__Main Auction Companies Who Hold Regular Auctions__

www.centurionservice.com

www.bigmedicalauctions.com

www.proxibid.com

www.dotmed.com

www.hibid.com

www.gsaauctions.gov

www.govplanet.com

www.mesauctions.com

www.govdeals.com

The third type of auction is a "Live On-Site Auction." Meaning there is an auctioneer present, and he verbally announces each item or lot number for sale. I am sure everyone has seen or heard a live auction either in person or on television.

First, the auctioneer will start the bidding at a specific dollar amount and will keep lowering that dollar amount until someone places the first bid. The auctioneer will, then, start to increase the bid until nobody is bidding anymore.

At that point, the auctioneer will begin to close the bidding by saying "Going once. Going twice.," and then will pause before saying, "Sold," or, "Going, going. Gone."

At that point, the item is considered sold and the auctioneer will move onto the next item for sale and the process repeats.

7

What Not to Buy at Auctions

When you view medical auctions, you will be overwhelmed at the amount of supplies available, but that doesn't mean you can buy any items.

Some items are more valuable than others and some items are not good to purchase. The nice aspect about medical auctions is that the catalog of products is visible for a week or two before the auction ends and that gives you plenty of time to research the products before you bid on them.

The best advice I can give you is to never buy any type of medical equipment from an auction that requires the item to run on electricity.

For example: an ultrasound machine. The reason is very simple and that is: *How do you know if it works or not?* The answer is: *You don't.*

Therefore, if you buy it and it doesn't work, you will have to pay a lot of money to have it repaired. Worse yet, maybe it has a software issue and can't be fixed. So, the most important rule of thumb is to never buy equipment that requires a power source to turn it on.

Keep in mind, that auction companies sell items, *"as is where is,"* which means you can't return the item if it is broken.

However, there is one exception to that rule. If the auction company shows a photo or photos of the equipment turned on, then the auction company is representing that the piece of equipment is working.

Therefore, you can purchase that item. Sometimes in the item description, the auction company will state that the unit or item powers on. This is also a representation that the piece of equipment is working and thus you can buy it. So, under those two scenarios, you can feel confident that the item is in good working condition and that you can purchase it.

8

Selling Wholesale Versus Retail

When you sell at wholesale, it means that you are buying medical supplies and then re-selling them to another medical broker who will, then, sell those products to a medical facility.

The medical facility is considered the "end user." The "end user" is the facility which buys the medical products for the surgeon who, then, uses the medical products in surgery.

When you are selling your products at wholesale to other medical brokers, what you basically are is a "middleman." You still make profit, but not as much as if you were to sell the medical products yourself to the "end user."

When you sell at retail, it is not the typical retail you are thinking about or use to seeing. What I mean by that is you don't open a storefront and have people walking into your store to buy medical products.

You are not a Walmart. Retail means that you would be selling your medical products yourself directly to the hospitals or surgery centers, also known as the "end user."

When you take this route to sell your medical supplies, you command more of a profit versus selling wholesale to other medical brokers, being that you are no longer the "middleman."

9

Selling Your
Medical Products to
Hospitals and Surgery Centers

When selling your medical products to hospitals and surgery centers, there is a process, so to speak, that you will need to follow.

This is to ensure that you get your list of products you have for sale to the correct person at the medical facility and to ensure that you get paid.

Step 1:

When you call a hospital or surgery center, most times, it is the Receptionist or Operator who answers. At that point, you ask to be transferred to the Materials Manager. If, by chance, the facility does not have a dedicated Materials Manager, then your next point-off contact is the Purchasing Department Manager for the operating room.

Once you are transferred and the designated person answers, you will repeat the following "candid speech:"

"My name is *(your name)* and my company is *(name of your company)*. My company specializes in obtaining surgical supplies from medical facilities that have closed or from facilities who have excess supplies. We, then, re-sell those supplies at a large discount to other medical facilities who are interested in saving money. If you are interested in viewing our inventory for sale, I'll just need your email to send you over our current inventory list".

If the Materials Manager or Purchasing Agent agrees to receive your inventory list, make sure you verify his or her email address, full spelling of their name, and the best contact phone number, so, that you can follow up properly.

Step 2:

When the hospital or surgery center is ready to place an order, they will provide you, through email or verbally, the items they want to purchase.

At that time, they will also give you a P.O. Number, also known as a Purchase Order Number). That number is extremely important, as it is the only way you will get paid from the medical facility.

If at the end of your conversation, the person has not provided you with the purchase order number, then make sure you ask for it and then repeat it back to the person to verify you have the number correctly.

You will be placing that P.O. Number on your company invoice which you will send to the Accounts Payable Department. We will get to that step shortly.

Step 3.

Verbally verify the products that the medical facility is ordering from you. Example: verify each product code and the manufacturer name, the quantities, and the prices.

Finally, verify the ship-to address with the department or contact name and then verify the Purchase Order Number. Ask if ground shipping is okay or would they prefer to pay for expedited shipping.

If the facility chooses expedited shipping, be sure to ask, specifically, if they want it to be overnight or second day shipping. The medical facility is responsible for the cost of any shipping method and that cost will be reflected on the invoice you send to them for payment.

Step 4.

Create your company invoice to include everything in Step 3. Below, I have provided a sample invoice that you can use as a template or you can create your own, but just make sure that you put all the information on your invoice that you see on my sample invoice below.

Your Company Name INVOICE

Remit Payment To:

INVOICE DATE: 07-10-2022

Your Company
Your Street
Your City, State and Zip code

SHIP TO:

PURCHASE ORDER NUMBER

John Doe Hospital
Street Address
City, State
Zip code

78443

Manufacturer Name	Product Code	Quantity	Unit Price	Total Price
Arthrex	AR-7200	2 boxes	$100.00	$200.00
Ethicon	HAR36	4 Units	$80.00	$320.00
			SHIPPING	$20.00
			TOTAL INVOICE AMOUNT	$540.00

Thank you for the business and please call if you have any questions.

Step 5:

Package the items that the facility purchased and place your company invoice inside the box. It is very important to place your invoice in the package or, otherwise, the facility may not know who sent the package and you may not get paid.

Double check their order to make sure that you have everything in the box that the hospital or surgery centered ordered.

Step 6:

Make two copies of your company's invoice that you placed inside the package. One copy, you will place into your "Awaiting Payment Folder" on your desk, also known as your "Accounts Receivables Folder." The other copy you will place in a standard number ten white envelope and send it to the Accounts Payable Department of the medical facility. See the sample address below:

Name of Medical Facility

ATTN: Accounts Payable Department

Street Address

City, State, Zip Code

Note: Most hospitals and surgery centers pay on net thirty. This means that they enter your payment into their computer system then send out your payment thirty days later.

Even though that is the "norm" in this business, some medical facilities pay sooner, and some pay a few days later.

Generally, I give a medical facility the thirty days and a little bit of a grace period. If I don't receive payment within forty-five days, I, then, call the Accounts Payable Department and provide the Purchase Order Number to inquire about paying the invoice.

Out of all my years in business, there was only one time that I didn't get paid by a medical facility which was due to them filing bankruptcy. So, the chances of you not getting paid by a medical facility are slim to none.

Remember, you are saving them money. Thus, they want to get you paid to keep you happy so that you will continue sending them lists of products to buy.

It's a win-win scenario for everyone.

10

Selling Your
Medical Products to
Other Medical Brokers

Now that you are in the business of buying and selling medical supplies, you are considered a "Medical Broker." That is your official title if you would like to have a title.

Before I get into the steps of how to sell to medical brokers, let's look at why you would choose to sell your medical products to another medical broker versus selling to a hospital or surgery center.

Let's say you have a large list of medical products which you send out to numerous hospitals and surgery centers. Maybe, a month or two months later, you still have items that no hospital or surgery center bought from you.

The main goal is to sell all your inventory and then re-invest your profits, or some of your profits, into buying larger amounts of inventory. That's called "flipping" your products and the more you flip, the more money you earn.

So, the last thing you want is for same unsold inventory to be sitting on your shelves month after month. That, in no way, benefits your company.

So, with that being said, you would contact other medical brokers in the industry to, hopefully, sell as much of your unsold inventory as you can. Just because you couldn't find a medical facility to buy some of your items, that doesn't mean another broker isn't able to find buyers.

Everybody in this industry has different buyers for different products. I am sure you have heard the phrase, "One person's junk is another person's treasure." That saying holds true for this type of business.

Example: you are sitting on ten boxes of a product from the manufacturer, Arthrex, and the product code is AR-7200. However, you just can't seem to find a medical facility who uses that specific product.

Thus, you can't sell it. However, maybe another medical broker has a hospital who uses that product on a regular basis. *If* that is the case, of course, the medical broker will offer to buy your ten boxes, because he or she already has a buyer for them.

So, in conclusion, yes, selling to your competitors is something you, sometimes, have to do in order to make more money by selling products you can't find buyers for.

Now, let's get into the steps you need to take in order to sell your products to other medical brokers.

*S*tep *1*:

Google search, "Medical Sales Brokers," or type into Google, "We buy medical supplies," to find medical brokers throughout the United States.

Contact via phone, not through email, as it's impersonal and you won't receive as much of an open reception. Further down below, I will provide you with a list of medical brokers that I have done millions of dollars in sales with over many years.

Whereas I can vouch that they are legit and honest businesspeople. You can, of course, find more brokers online, but if I have not listed them below, then, I haven't done enough business with them to say that I can trust them with all certainty.

There is nothing wrong with finding other medical brokers to potentially do business with. However, I strongly advise that if you take that route, you ask for payment upfront prior to sending the medical broker the supplies that he or she purchased from you.

Step 2:

Almost all medical brokers will be receptive to you emailing them a list of the supplies that you have for sale. In the event that the medical brokers extend you offers to purchase some of your items, and if you like the offers, you will, then, need to explain that you would need payment *upfront* prior to shipping the items.

If the broker is not willing to do that then, at that point, you will have to decide as to whether you want to trust that this person will pay you once he or she receives your items.

You always have the option of offering a compromise which is to send half of the products and then, once you receive payment, you will send out the other half.

Yes, it will take longer to get paid in full but, at the same time, it will help establish trust between both of you. On the devil's advocate side, if you don't get paid, then you only lost half of the money. Basically, it cuts your potential losses.

Now, here is the exception to the rule of receiving payment first prior to sending products to another medical broker. The medical brokers I am listing below are, as I said previously, people whom I can vouch for and whom you can trust. Some of them have no issue with paying you upfront prior to you shipping them the supplies. Yet some of them require you to first ship out the products to them and then they will send you payment anywhere between seven and thirty days.

I advise you to discuss payment terms with them via phone so that you know what to expect. It needs to be pointed out that all the brokers' names whom I am now going to give you are multi-millionaires and wouldn't screw you out of a penny.

They each realize that suppliers, such as yourself, are of great importance to their company. After all, the more products they buy from you, the more money they earn and thus they wouldn't burn your bridge.

It's common sense for them!

Below, I will provide you with a list of medical brokers that I have done millions of dollars in sales with over many years:

Company   Ringle Medical Supply

Contact   Sal Panetta

Telephone   715-370-5753

Company   Paper Street Medical

Contact   Adam Woronecki

Telephone   954-319-7723

Company   Palm Harbor Medical

Contact   Gary Van Meer

Telephone   800-301-5376

Company   West Coast Medical Supplies

Contact   Randy Ware

Telephone   800-565-6385

Company   MTM Medical

Contact   Matt McRoberts

Telephone   561-746-0828

Company	Surgical Product Solutions
Contact	Rocco
Telephone	412-564-1280

Company	eSutures
Contact	Anthony
Telephone	844-788-8737

Company	SH Medical
Contact	Marcello
Telephone	305-406-2222

Company	Medical Materials
Contact	Jessica
Telephone	561-375-7857

11

Developing an Excel Spreadsheet of Your Inventory

Whether you are going to sell your medical supplies to hospitals, surgery centers, or to medical brokers, it is absolutely necessary that you create an Excel Spreadsheet of your inventory.

I realize that there are other ways to create and list out your inventory, but Excel is the easiest to use and it is the most used in the medical industry. So, let's stick to what works the best for all practical purposes.

When you are sending your inventory list to a hospital or surgery center, the Excel Spreadsheet must contain the following:

1) Manufacturer Name
2) Product Code
3) Quantity Available
4) Expiration Date (if applicable)
5) Product Description
6) Price you are Selling Each Product for

Note: The expiration date would only apply if the product were an implant or disposable. Instruments don't have expiration dates due to the fact that they are cleaned and re-sterilized after each surgical procedure.

Below is an Excel Spreadsheet sample of exactly how it should look when sending your inventory to a hospital or surgery center.

When sending the Excel Spreadsheet to a medical broker, it is important that you remove your pricing, because you want the medical broker to make you an offer. You can always try to negotiate up in price if you are not satisfied with their offers.

The main reason you don't want to send a list to a medical broker with your prices is because it's quite possible that they may offer you more money than what you are asking for the product.

MANUFACTURER	PRODUCT CODE	QUANTITY	BOX OR UNIT	EXPIRATION DATE
Ethicon	ECR45G	1	BOX OF 12	EXPIRED
Ethicon	CDH25A	9	UNITS	EXPIRED
Ethicon	HARHD20	5	UNITS	EXPIRED
Medtronic	8225825	7	UNITS	EXPIRED
Medtronic	23-112-1	5	UNITS	EXPIRED
Covidien	EGIA45AMT	3	UNITS	EXPIRED
Covidien	LF1744	1	UNITS	EXPIRED
Hologic	NS2013US	1	UNIT	EXPIRED
Endocre, Inc	PCS-24	2	UNITS	EXPIRED
Spectranetics	500-303	2	UNITS	EXPIRED
Lumenis	0641-047-01	4	UNITS	2022-07-23
Lumenis	0641-055-01	2	UNITS	2022-06-23

PRODUCT DESCRIPTION

reloads
curved intraluminal stapler, 25mm
harmonic HD 1000i shears
incrementing probe with standard prass tip
aquamantys 6.0 bipolar sealer
endo gia articulating reloads with tri-staple technology, 45mm, medium/thick
ligasure maryland jaw laparoscopic sealer/divider
novasure advanced
perCryo cryoprobe
GlideLight laser sheath, size 16F
SlimLine 1000 fiber delivery device
SlimLine 550 fiber delivery device

95

12

Selling Your
Medical Products Online

Some of you may choose or prefer to sell your products online, which is a very viable means to build your business.

By selling online, you will not need to contact hospitals or surgery centers to sell products. One beneficial aspect in doing so is that online sales you get paid immediately versus selling to a hospital or surgery center and waiting thirty days to get paid.

In this business, it is the "norm" to give medical facilities a net thirty payment term. Very few medical facilities will pay you upfront for medical supplies and the reason for this is that the manufacturers whom the medical facility is generally buying from gives almost all medical facilities a thirty day net payment term.

The two best places to sell your medical products online are on the following sites:

1) www.ebay.com
2) www.dotmed.com

Let me explain the difference between the two of them. eBay has a higher volume of buyers. Therefore, you will sell more products faster. However, people in general, shop on eBay to save money and, thus, they seem to want lower prices. Dotmed has less users shopping on the site, but on the flip side, they pay higher prices.

Furthermore, eBay has more of a boat load of restrictions when it comes to selling medical products. Dotmed, on the other hand, has pretty much no restrictions and could care less what medical products you sell on their site.

My suggestion is to do a combination of the two sites. The benefit of doing so broadens your buyer base and gives your company more exposure.

Another benefit is that if you have any medical products removed off eBay due to a policy violation, you can then re-list that product on Dotmed.

A policy violation is simply when eBay removes items off eBay that they don't allow to be sold. It is *not* against the law, but rather just an eBay policy regarding what items they allow or don't allow to be sold on their site.

13

Pricing Your Medical Products

Once you have determined whether or not you will be selling your medical supplies wholesale or retail, you, now, need to determine the selling prices of your medical products.

There are many avenues to find medical products for sale online, which you can use to price your products. All medical products have either a product code or model number. This is what you will need to research your product.

Some manufacturers of medical products may use different terminology other than the word, "Product Code," on their products. For example: they may use the word, "Reference Number (REF#)," or, "Catalog Number." All of which essentially have the same meaning or purpose, which is to identify the product.

Once you have located the product code, you can use the following avenues to locate the product online for the purpose of determining the selling price.

1)   www.google.com

2)   www.ebay.com

3)   www.dotmed.com

In addition to the aforementioned, you may also check some of your competitor's websites (including the medical brokers' websites that I listed prior in this guidebook, as many of them have thousands of products for sale on their website).

This can be very beneficial being that your competitors have been in the medical sales business for years and they have spent countless dollars researching prices in which they can sell their products to hospitals and surgery centers.

So basically, they have already determined the max price in which the products will sell for on the secondary market. The term, "secondary market," means that the hospital or surgery center is buying products from medical brokers, such as yourself, versus buying directly from the medical product manufacturer.

Here is an example. If a hospital calls the manufacturer, Arthrex, to order a product and, let's say the product code is, AR-13990, which is called a Scorpion Suture Passer, the hospital will pay $3,500.00USD from the manufacturer.

However, if the hospital buys the same product on the secondary market from a broker, such as yourself, the price may be $2,500.00USD; saving the hospital $1,000.00USD.

Of course, you could sell it for less if you choose and that is something you can determine based on how much you paid for the product.

The majority of hospitals and surgery centers in America are open to buying medical products on the secondary market for the main purpose of saving money.

Below are some of the medical brokers throughout the United States who have built large successful companies and their websites will be extremely helpful in determining selling prices for your medical products.

1)   www.palmharbormedical.com

2)   www.esutures.com

3)   www.westcmr.com

4)   www.medicalmaterials.com

5)   www.shopsps.com

14

Inspecting Your Products
Before Selling

Quality control is very important when selling medical products.

The last thing you want to do is send a faulty or damaged product to one of your buyers. Once you receive medical products which you have purchased from a hospital, surgery center, or from a medical auction, you will, then, want to inspect them.

If you are buying instruments, you will want to make sure that they are not broken. If you are buying implants or disposables, you will want to check the packaging to make sure that there are no tears or punctures to the packing, which would then, mean that the sterility of the product has been jeopardized.

If you are buying equipment that requires power, you will want to plug it in to make sure that it works. The last thing you will ever want to do is send one of your customers a defective product. In doing so, you risk losing that person or facility as a repeat customer. It is very important to maintain an impeccable reputation.

In fact, it is always a good idea to register your business with your local better business bureau and do your best to maintain an "A" or "A+" rating. In doing so, you can, then, represent that on your website (if you choose to build a website) and on any marketing material you send to potential customers.

15

Rotation of Inventory

Rotation of inventory only applies to implants and disposables being they have expiration dates.

Assuming you keep your inventory on shelves. *If* you have more than one box of any specific product code and they have different expiration dates, you want to make sure that the products with the shortest expiration dates are towards the front of the shelf.

This way, you sell it first before it completely expires. Whenever you have products that have expired, (past the expiration date), keep in mind that they still have value to international hospitals and surgery centers.

They of course can't be sold to any medical facilities within the United States. There is, actually, a huge market for expired medical products in foreign countries. Reason being most can't afford to buy products with good expiration dates from the actual manufacturer.

Therefore, many international hospitals and doctors look to eBay or other websites to buy expired items. The best avenue to sell expired medical products is on eBay or Dotmed.

16

Scams to Avoid

There seems to be a scam for everything in life and selling medical supplies is no exception.

If you choose to sell your medical products online, you will come across someone trying to scam you sooner or later, so, here is what to be aware of.

Let's say you are selling products on eBay, and you find a potential buyer has sent you a message. One of the biggest scams is that the buyer will offer to send you a cashier's check and then is requesting that he has a friend or driver pick up the product from you in person.

Of course, your first thought is this must be legit, because a cashier's check is from a bank. You would be incorrect in thinking that.

Truth be told, a bank may cash the cashier's check on the spot, but technically it still takes three to seven business days for the cashier's check to, actually, clear. If the cashier's check "bounces," then the bank will come after you for the money. By that time, the person has already picked up the product(s) from you in person.

To avoid this scam, you can tell the person that he or she may pick up the product or products in person, but you will be requiring payment in the form of "cash only."

The next scam to be aware of is that you will receive emails saying things like, "Your PayPal account has been temporarily restricted," or that, "PayPal needs you to verify information."

You will, then, see a link in the email that the person who sent you the email wants you to click on. Once you click on that link, it will ask you your log in information.

If you were to provide that information, you are essentially giving that person your log in information and password. Before you know it, all your money will be taken out of PayPal.

So, to avoid this scam, simply call PayPal if you receive any type of email regarding your PayPal account. Customer service will, then, advise you as to whether they need any information to verify anything pertaining to your account.

17

Bookkeeping and
Record Keeping

Good bookkeeping and record keeping are vital to operating a successful business.

It allows you to gauge where your business sits financially, as well as, which medical products are selling and which ones are not.

It also helps to determine growth projections for your business. Sound business decisions should be based on where you stand financially. This includes but is not limited to decisions, such as, taking on an employee or multiple employees, buying more inventory, or moving to a larger office or warehouse.

There are several aspects of bookkeeping and record keeping that you need to be cognizant of, as they will affect your business.

I, personally, suggest having an accounting firm handle this part of the business for you, whereas, the accounting firm will guide you with the records they require you to provide on a regular basis.

However, if you are capable of doing the bookkeeping and record keeping yourself, then you will save money versus hiring an accountant.

*N*umber *1*:

Establishing Bookkeeping Procedures

Basic bookkeeping starts on a day-by-day, sale-by-sale level. Software programs make much of this work more simple if you are versed in using them.

Whether you are using a software program or ding the bookkeeping manually, you'll need to keep a journal of sales and cash receipts. This will allow you to see your sales totals, know which items were sold in cash or on credit, and keep track of when you received payments.

At the end of each day, you will enter your daily sales total into your sales journal. If you are using sales invoices, you can keep accounts for each sale and customer updated by posting entries to the accounts receivable ledger.

Make sure you file all customer invoices by number. Keeping a copy for yourself and providing one to your customer so that either of you can reference the invoice if questions arise.

You will also be keeping and maintaining a cash disbursement journal, also known as, an expense journal. This will allow you to know how much you are spending and to whom you are paying the money.

*N*umber *2*:

Cash or Accrual Accounting System

Two basic accounting methods are the cash method and the accrual method. With the cash method, you record income only when you receive it from your customers. You will also be recording when you pay out cash or write a check.

This system is very simple; however, the problem is that, now a days, most businesses are not a cash only business. Many customers would prefer to pay with a credit card, which when using a cash accounting system, it doesn't work as well nor as accurate.

Now a days, the accrual accounting method is more commonly used. With the accrual method, every transaction is recorded when it occurs regardless as to if it is cash or credit.

This is a more accurate system especially, now a days, when most of your customers, (hospitals and surgery centers), who, generally, will pay you net thirty days from the date of sale.

According to the IRS, you must use the accrual system if you are maintaining inventory. In your case, you would have medical products on your shelf which you are holding to sell and thus is considered inventory.

With that being said, and to meet IRS guidelines, you would be using the accrual accounting method.

18

Accounting Software

When choosing an accounting software for your business, it should be one that is easy to use, (user friendly), and include features relevant to your business.

If you have an accountant with whom you are working with, make sure to talk to that person about the software program you plan to use.

Reason being, you want to make sure your accountant is familiar with the program and that it is compatible with his or her computer.

In conclusion, when it comes to taxes and accounting, I suggest talking to a person who specializes in those areas.

Online Live Training
Course Available

Although this guidebook contains everything you need to know in order to start your own business buying and selling medical supplies, I have found that some people would like further training. Therefore, I, personally, offer a 6 hour live online training course every other month for a very minimal fee.

On the next page of this guidebook, you will find the course registration page. Simply tear it out of this guidebook, complete the information and send the form to the address provided on the page.

Available course dates are listed online on my website at www.sellmedsupplies.com. Registration is also available online.

Thank you,

David Powers

Online Live Training Registration

If you would like to attend a 6 hour online live training course on how to buy and sell medical supplies, simply complete the form on the following page and return it with payment to the below address. Once your registration form is received, you will be contacted with more information. You may also register for this course online at www.sellmedsupplies.com.

The 6-hour online training course fee is only $750.00USD.

Please do not send cash. Payment must be made either by money order or cashier's check. Please make payable to David Powers and mail payment along with your completed registration page to:

David Powers

1870 N. Corporate Lakes Blvd, # 267698

Weston, FL 33326

Online Live Training Registration

PLEASE PRINT NEATLY

First and Last Name:

_____

Address:

_____

City: State: Zip Code:

_____   _____   _____

Email Address:

_____

Telephone Number: Preferred Course Date:
                                    (Course dates are listed online
                                    at www.sellmedsupplies.com)

_____   _____

119

For more information on how you can start your own business
buying and selling medical supplies or how you can attend
an online live training course with David, please visit

www.sellmedsupplies.com

Printed in the USA
CPSIA information can be obtained
at www.ICGtesting.com
LVHW101129250923
759237LV00005B/247